MW00436417

My HOLY HOUR
St. Therese of Lisieux

A Devotional Journal

Season: _____

Date: _____

Belongs to: _____

My Holy Hour - St. Therese of Lisieux is part of the *My Holy Hour Devotional Journal Series*. While all journals will have some similar structure and intent, each one will have minor changes to make it unique. Cover image depicts a stained glass of *St. Therese of Lisieux*.

Go to our website for a free copy of
How to Use a Prayer Journal during Holy Hour
www.HolyHourBooks.com

Holy Hour Books
P.O. Box 430577
Houston, TX 77243

My Holy Hour Devotional Journals

Copyright © 2017 Vikk Simmons
All rights reserved worldwide

Cover Image Under License

ISBN-13: 978-1-941303-55-9
ISBN-10: 1-941303-55-2

First Printing: 2017

Holy Hour Books is an imprint of Ordinary Matters Publishing.

All rights reserved. No part of this book may be reproduced in any form or by any electronic or mechanical means, including information storage and retrieval systems, without permission in writing from the author, except in the case of brief quotations used in critical articles or reviews. This means that you cannot record or photocopy any material, ideas, or tips that are provided in this book. Requests for permission should be addressed to the publisher.

Printed in the United States of America

Oh my God! I offer Thee all my actions of this day for the intentions and for the glory of the Sacred Heart of Jesus. I desire to sanctify every beat of my heart, my every thought, my simplest works, by uniting them to Its infinite merits, and I wish to make reparation for my sins by casting them into the furnace of Its Merciful Love.

O my God! I ask of Thee for myself and for those whom I hold dear, the grace to fulfill perfectly Thy Holy Will, to accept for love of Thee the joys and sorrows of this passing life, so that we may one day be united together in heaven for all Eternity."

—Morning Prayer by St. Therese of Lisieux

Why Keep a Holy Hour

"First, the Holy Hour is not a devotion; it is a sharing in the work of redemption... our Lord asked: 'Could you not watch one hour with Me?'. In other words, he asked for an hour of reparation to combat the hour of evil; an hour of victimal union with the Cross to overcome the anti-love of sin.

Secondly, the only time Our Lord asked the Apostles for anything was the night he went into his agony... As often in the history of the Church since that time, evil was awake, but the disciples were asleep. That is why there came out of His anguished and lonely Heart the sigh: 'Could you not watch one hour with me?' Not for an hour of activity did He plead, but for an hour of companionship.

The third reason I keep up the Holy Hour is to grow more and more into his likeness. As Paul puts it: 'We are transfigured into his likeness, from splendor to splendor.' We become like that which we gaze upon. Looking into a sunset, the face takes on a golden glow. Looking at the Eucharistic Lord for an hour transforms the heart in a mysterious way as the face of Moses was transformed after his companionship with God on the mountain. Something happens to us similar to that which happened to the disciples at Emmaus. On Easter Sunday afternoon when the Lord met them, he asked why they were so gloomy. After spending some time in his presence, and hearing again the secret of spirituality - 'The Son of Man must suffer to enter into his Glory'" - their time with him ended and their "hearts were on fire." — Bishop Fulton Sheen

How to Keep a Holy Hour

"I have found that it takes some time to catch fire in prayer. This has been one of the advantages of the daily Hour. It is not so brief as to prevent the soul from collecting itself and shaking off the multitudinous distractions of the world. Sitting before the Presence is like a body exposing itself before the sun to absorb its rays. Silence in the Hour is a tete-a-tete with the Lord. In those moments, one does not so much pour out written prayers, but listening takes its place. We do not say: 'Listen, Lord, for Thy servant speaks,' but 'Speak, Lord, for Thy servant heareth.'"— Bishop Fulton Sheen

"Know also that you will probably gain more by praying fifteen minutes before the Blessed Sacrament than by all the other spiritual exercises of the day. True, Our Lord hears our prayers anywhere, for He has made the promise, 'Ask, and you shall receive,' but He has revealed to His servants that those who visit Him in the Blessed Sacrament will obtain a more abundant measure of grace." — St. Alphonsus Liguori

Holy Hour Pages

"The purpose of the Holy Hour is to encourage deep personal encounter with Christ."

— *Bishop Fulton Sheen*

HOLY HOUR QUOTES

Prayer to St. Therese of Lisieux

O little St. Therese of the Child Jesus, who during your short life on earth became a mirror of angelic purity, of love strong as death, and of wholehearted abandonment to God, now that you rejoice in the reward of your virtues, cast a glance of pity on me as I leave all things in ;your hands. Make my troubles your own—speak a word for me to our Lady Immaculate, whose flower of special love you were—to that Queen of Heaven "who smiled on you at the dawn of life." Beg her as the Queen of the Heart of Jesus to obtain for me by her powerful intercession, the grace I yearn for so ardently at this moment, and that she join with it a blessing that may strengthen me during life. Defend me at the hour of death, and lead me straight on to a happy eternity. Amen.

"In times of aridity when I am incapable of praying, of practicing virtue, I see little opportunities, mere trifles, to give pleasure to Jesus; for instance a smile, a pleasant word when inclined to be silent and to show weariness. If I find no opportunities, I at least tell Him again and again that I love Him; that is not difficult and it keeps alive the fire in my heart. Even though this fire of love might seem extinct I would still throw little straws upon the embers and I am certain it would rekindle.

— St. Therese of Lisieux

Record Your Favorite Quotes Here

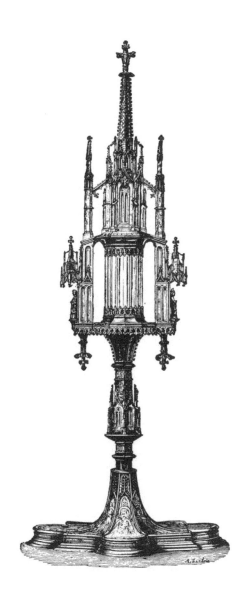

REFLECTIONS

Personal Index

_____ *Pgs* ____

_____ *Pgs* ____

_____ *Pgs* ____

_____ *Pgs* ____

_____ *Pgs* ____

_____ *Pgs* ____

_____ *Pgs* ____

_____ *Pgs* ____

_____ *Pgs* ____

_____ *Pgs* ____

_____ *Pgs* ____

_____ *Pgs* ____

_____ *Pgs* ____

_____ *Pgs* ____

_____ *Pgs* ____

_____ *Pgs* ____

_____ *Pgs* ____

_____ *Pgs* ____

_____ *Pgs* ____

_____ *Pgs* ____

_____ *Pgs* ____

_____ *Pgs* ____

_____ *Pgs* ____

HOLY HOUR JOURNALS

Thank you for your interest in *Holy Hour Journals*. Discover more about using journals to deepen your prayer life by going to our website and getting a free copy of

How to Use a Prayer Journal during Holy Hour
www.HolyHourBooks.com

The Holy Hour Devotional Journal Series has been created to help Catholics from all walks of life to discover, explore, and enjoy the many rewards from a deeper connection to Christ.

Like our Facebook Page:
https://www.facebook.com/HolyHourBooks